The Russian Revolution

A Captivating Guide to the February and October Revolutions and the Rise of the Soviet Union Led by Vladimir Lenin and the Bolsheviks

Free Bonus from Captivating History (Available for a Limited time)

Hi History Lovers!

Now you have a chance to join our exclusive history list so you can get your first history ebook for free as well as discounts and a potential to get more history books for free! Simply visit the link below to join.

Captivatinghistory.com/ebook

Also, make sure to follow us on:

Twitter: @Captivhistory

Facebook: Captivating History:@captivatinghistory

Contents

Introduction

The Russian Revolution of 1917 was a monumental event in global history, and its 100th anniversary, in 2017, was commemorated around the world. While attitudes towards Lenin and the establishment of the world's first communist state by the Bolshevik Party are divided, the fact that it was a major historical event is undeniable. In many ways, the centennial was far more subdued in Russia, which regards the revolution as a traumatic event that divided the country and is keen to promote a sense of national unity. Despite this, historians from Russia and across the world have published books marking the anniversary and it is clear that the Russian Revolution remains of interest to the general public to this day.

The Russian Revolution of 1917—perhaps more accurately the revolutions of 1917—were a series of complex events involving a large number of key individuals. Some of these individuals, such as Kerensky, Lenin, and Trotsky, are at the heart of the narrative. Others, such as Kornilov, emerge briefly and prominently and then fade away. This book will explain the motivations of individuals and the causes behind the chain of events that led to the downfall of the Romanov monarchy all the way to the elevation of Lenin as the head of the Russian government. By doing so, it aims to cast doubt on the belief that Lenin's rise to power was inevitable, at the same time highlighting the key role Lenin played throughout 1917 to influence events.

Note on Dates

In 1917, Russia used the Old Style or Julian Calendar, which is thirteen days behind the New Style or Gregorian Calendar. In February 1918, as part of reforms to modernize Russia, Lenin's government switched from Old Style to New Style Calendar.

Dates in this book before Lenin's reform are given in the Old Style. Dates given after February 1918 are provided in the New Style. While this is not particularly consistent, it is a standard commonly used by historians writing about revolutionary Russia.

Chapter 1 – Twilight of the Tsars

On 20 July 1914, a large crowd gathered on St. Petersburg's Palace Square in front of the Winter Palace. On the balcony stood Nicholas II, Emperor and Tsar of All the Russias, in a military uniform glistening with service decorations. The previous day, Kaiser Wilhelm II of Germany, the Tsar's cousin, had issued a declaration of war against Russia and France. In response, the Russian Tsar announced before the assembled masses that Russia was prepared to defend herself against enemy aggression, vowing to drive the Germans out of Russian territory. Cries of 'Hurrah' echoed around the crowd, men waved their hats in the air, and the Russian people rallied behind their Tsar, anticipating a swift victory over the insolent Germans.

The fervor for war in Russia, as elsewhere in Europe, was genuine. Russia had mobilized its army against Austria-Hungary in order to defend its ally Serbia, a fellow Orthodox Slavic nation. Some optimists dreamed that in the ensuing war, Russia would finally manage to capture Constantinople, a foreign policy objective for Russian rulers ever since it fell to the Ottoman Empire in 1453. Although the popularity of the Romanov dynasty was in decline as Russia entered the twentieth century, the old cry of 'For Tsar and Fatherland' once again rang out across St. Petersburg and the empire. The Tsar remained, in the eyes of many, the embodiment of Russia. The State Duma, Russia's parliament, stopped meeting in order to form a united front to support the war effort. This was no time for petty political arguments.

At the very beginning, the war seemed to go well for Russia. Germany expected it would take six weeks for Russia to fully mobilize its army, during which it expected to have defeated France. Instead, through a gargantuan effort, the Russian army managed to mobilize in a mere ten days. This completely negated the Schlieffen Plan, which had been developed to ensure that Germany would avoid fighting a two-front war against France and Russia. The First and Second Russian Armies under Generals Rennenkampf and Samsonov, more than 300,000 men in total, began to march through eastern Prussia virtually unopposed, throwing the German High Command into panic. The German Eighth Army of 150,000 men was formed under the command of the retired General Paul von Hindenburg, with Erich von Ludendorff as chief of staff.

The rapid mobilization of Russian forces, although impressive, was carried out at a significant cost. The two Russian armies marched separately across difficult terrain and were unable to support each other. Supply trains lagged behind the army. Russian soldiers were not fully equipped as they prepared for battle. Not every soldier in the ranks was issued with a rifle, and unarmed soldiers were expected to pick up the rifles of their comrades who had fallen in battle. Those fortunate men who had rifles did not have enough ammunition. Due to limited firepower, the Russian infantry would be obliged to engage in reckless bayonet charges in an effort to conserve their ammunition and inflict damage on the enemy with cold steel.

Hindenburg and Ludendorff effectively exploited the difficulties the Russian army faced. Faced with the two-pronged Russian attack, the Germans moved corps and divisions from one part of the front to the other by railroad. At the Battle of Tannenberg between 13 and 17 August (26-30 August N.S.), the German command decided to concentrate its resources against the Second Army, which managed to advance quicker than the First Army. Most of Samsonov's Second

Army eventually found itself encircled with no line of retreat. On the penultimate day of the battle, Samsonov committed suicide as his men surrendered to the enemy. At the end of the battle, 92,000 Russian soldiers were taken into captivity and almost as many were killed or wounded. Arguably of greater importance were the 350 Russian artillery pieces captured by the Germans.

After annihilating the Second Army, the Germans turned their attention towards Rennenkampf's First Army. Reinforced by two corps from the Western Front, the German Eighth Army attacked Rennenkampf at the Masurian Lakes between 19 August – 2 September (1-15 September N.S.). In this battle the Russians suffered a strategic defeat which forced it to abandon any offensive plans and withdraw from German territory. The Russian army lost 250,000 men as well as a large part of its military equipment.

The setbacks at Tannenberg and the Masurian Lakes were major blows to the Russian military effort. The Russians were forced to retreat five hundred miles, abandoning large stretches of territory in Poland, Belarus, and the Baltic. This proved immensely damaging to morale both in the army and at the home front. In an effort to increase morale, despite the opposition of his ministers, in September 1915 Tsar Nicholas decided to leave his capital and assume command at General Headquarters. By making such a momentous decision, the Tsar was placing responsibility for the war effort into his own hands.

The Tsar's presence at headquarters appeared to have the desired effect, as the performance of the Russian army improved substantially in 1916. Morale increased among the men. The shortages in military supplies were being addressed now that factories all across the country were tasked with providing munitions for the war. Pioneering creeping barrage tactics, and with a well-supplied army at his disposal, General Alexei Brusilov launched a devastating offensive against the unsuspecting Austro-Hungarian army in Galicia. The Austrians lost over a million men as Slavic units of the Austrian army flooded across Russian lines to change their allegiance. The Habsburg Empire was dealt a mortal blow from which it would never recover.

Despite its many successes, the Brusilov Offensive was an ultimate failure, since Russian forces in the northern sector of the Eastern Front failed to maintain pressure on the German lines. This allowed the German command scope to grant the Austrian Emperor's request for reinforcements to bolster his deteriorating position. The German troops managed to successfully hold off Brusilov's attacks before launching a counter-offensive to drive Brusilov back behind his initial lines. In the final reckoning the offensive cost the Russian army almost a million men to little effect. Nevertheless, the performance was a significant improvement on previous years and the Russian command had high hopes that the war would shift in their favor in 1917.

Whatever hopes the Tsar and his generals had for 1917 were not reflected in the capital. While the Tsar remained at headquarters, the situation in the home front deteriorated. The need to supply the army with food and equipment caused shortages in Russia, which in turn led to inflation as the prices of everyday goods skyrocketed. The efforts to increase production in the factories also had a negative effect. While factory owners made large profits, workers were forced to work for long hours in poor conditions for low wages. The situation was exploited by socialist politicians who denounced the government for fighting an imperialist war and called for peace with the Germans—after all, the rank-and-file of the German army were also fellow workers forced into uniform by their imperialist overlords.

In Petrograd, the tsarist government did not only face opposition from socialist revolutionaries, but came under fire from political factions all across the political spectrum. The State Duma reassembled to debate the government's mishandling of the war effort. Upon his departure from the capital, the Tsar entrusted day-to-day government affairs to his wife, Tsarina Alexandra. The Tsarina had been a princess of the German Grand Duchy of Hesse, and many Russians of all backgrounds had suspicions that she had German sympathies. In a celebrated speech in 1916, the liberal politician Pavel Milyukov accused the government's persecution of the war as "either incompetence or treason."

Although the allegations of treason against Alexandra were largely the result of propaganda, the Tsarina was fiercely protective of her imperial powers and resisted attempts from private industry to encroach on tsarist prerogatives. As a result, efforts by the Military Industrial Committee, set up in 1915 by business leaders to support the war effort, were regarded with suspicion. Keen to avoid ministers from consolidating too much power in their hands, Alexandra dismissed those who seemed intent on taking an active political role against the monarchy's wishes. As a result, there were four different prime ministers over the course of 1916, a situation which monarchist Duma deputy Vladimir Purishkevich described as "ministerial leapfrog." Issuing orders one day and counter-orders the next, the government in Petrograd was in a state of complete disorder.

One individual who appeared to be constantly present at Alexandra's side was the peasant monk Grigory Rasputin. Rasputin had been a frequent visitor to the imperial court following the birth of Tsarevich Alexei, the heir to the throne, in 1904. After four daughters, Tsar Nicholas finally had his male heir, but the young tsarevich was a hemophiliac and constantly required supervision and medical attention. As doctors despaired over Alexei's condition, only Rasputin seemed to have the ability to stop the bleeding. Keen to ensure the survival of her son for personal and political reasons, Alexandra ensured that Rasputin was never far away.

The presence of Rasputin at court troubled ministers and family members alike. Unsurprisingly, noble court grandees found the Siberian peasant's speech and manners repulsive. The closeness between the Tsarina and the man whom she referred to in letters to her husband as 'our friend' sparked scandalous rumors across the capital and beyond. Satirical cartoons visualized the rumors that

Rasputin was having sexual relations with the Tsarina and her ladies-in-waiting—the propagation of which Rasputin appeared to actively encourage. Already, in 1912, Speaker of the State Duma Mikhail Rodzianko warned the Tsar that "no revolutionary propaganda could achieve as much as Rasputin's mere presence at court," presenting Nicholas with a pile evidence of Rasputin's immoral behavior. On several occasions Rasputin was sent away, but he always found a way back. With the Tsar away from his capital, it seemed as though Rasputin was directing affairs of government alongside the Tsarina.

Over the years numerous plots had been conjured by state ministries to assassinate Rasputin, but they had all been abandoned through lack of will. Eventually Prince Felix Yusupov decided to take the matter into his own hands. Married to the Tsar's niece, Yusupov persuaded Grand Duke Dmitri Pavlovich to join the plot. Dmitri had a close relationship with the Tsar, his first cousin, but had been disillusioned by the way in which the war was being conducted. Vladimir Purishkevich, who had spoken out against Rasputin's influence in Duma sessions on several occasions, was also a willing member of the conspiracy.

It is impossible to know exactly what happened on the night of 16-17 December when the plot was carried out, since the eyewitness accounts by the perpetrators differ significantly from each other. While Yusupov became a celebrity in the western world for his role in Rasputin's death, in later years Grand Duke Dmitri seemed troubled by guilt. It appears that upon arriving at Yusupov's palace on the Moika river, Rasputin was first supplied with poisoned cakes and wine, which failed to have the desired effect. After some time, Yusupov shot at Rasputin, who fell motionless. When Yusupov approached Rasputin, the latter sprung up and wrestled him to the ground. With great difficulty Yusupov freed himself, whereupon Purishkevich fired several shots at Rasputin's head, which finally killed him.

The operation had taken much longer than anticipated, and the assassins were keen to dispose of the body as quickly as possible. It was already 5am and the darkness was already fading. After driving a short distance, the body was thrown into the Malaya Nevka river. In their hurry, the conspirators had forgotten to attach weights to hold the body down. News of the assassination spread across Petrograd quickly when Rasputin's bloodied body was discovered floating in the river beneath the ice. Yusupov and his co-conspirators believed that by removing Rasputin the monarchy could be saved and public opinion would be satisfied. Subsequent events were to prove otherwise.

Chapter 2 – The Midnight Train

By the end of 1916, increasingly severe economic problems faced at the home front by the people of Petrograd translated into a series of mass strikes and street demonstrations. While strikes were commonplace throughout the war, the ones at the beginning of 1917 were unprecedented in their size, scale, and militancy. On 9 January, more than 140,000 workers went on strike to commemorate the events of Bloody Sunday twelve years prior, when peaceful demonstrations were suppressed by Cossack troops on Palace Square in front of the Winter Palace. These events had launched the Revolution of 1905, a year-long series of demonstrations and protests against the Tsarist state across the entire country, resulting in concessions from Nicholas II, which included the establishment of the State Duma. Nicholas nevertheless managed to survive, though the imperial family decided to move out of the Winter Palace and live in the Alexander Palace in Tsarskoe Selo.

Although some workers were persuaded to return to work by promises of higher wages, by mid-February more than 100,000 workers remained on the streets. On 18 February 1917, 20,000 workers from the Putilov Arms Factory in Petrograd—which had made crucial contributions to supplying the Russian army with much-needed munitions—went on strike because their managers had denied them a pay increase. This triggered similar demonstrations in other factories as workers found it increasingly difficult to afford basic foodstuffs as prices continued to increase.

On 19 February, in an effort to ameliorate the economic shortages not only in Petrograd but across the country, the government announced the introduction of food rationing, which would begin in March. The policy had the opposite effect as intended, as people in Petrograd rushed to buy goods while they were still available and unrationed. These disturbances were amplified on 23 February, as Petrograd's womenfolk marked International Women's Day with demands for equal rights. As many as 500,000 people were on the streets for a range of different causes, but it was evident that all hoped for a change in the status quo. The police successfully fought to contain the disturbances, but it was clear that the maintenance of order in the capital was hanging by a thread.

On 25 February, the Tsar issued an order for General Sergei Khabalov, the commander of the Petrograd garrison, to suppress the demonstrations with rifle fire. On the following day, Khabalov reported to the Tsar that some units refused to carry out orders to fire at the crowds and instead joined them. The workers, recognizing that rank-and-file soldiers were of humble backgrounds, appealed to the soldiers and persuaded them that there was no point in fighting and dying for the Tsar's imperialist war aims. This was the first case of open mutiny in the Petrograd military garrison, which amounted to 170,000 men.

For much of Russian history, the army was a bastion of the monarchy that could be called upon to protect the state against revolution. However, as a result of the terrible losses suffered by the Russian army over the course of the war, the social composition of the Russian army had changed dramatically. It is estimated that by the beginning of 1917, 70 percent of the officer class—usually consisting of aristocrats—was of peasant origin. While the Russian peasantry had traditionally been supportive of the tsarist state, attitudes began to change at the end of the 19th century. Previous elections had shown that most peasants favored the agrarian socialist policies of the Socialist Revolutionary Party. This meant that many regiments that were ordered to suppress the revolutionaries decided to join the masses instead.

The breakdown of military discipline while Russia was engaged in a deadly war caused great anxiety among Russia's political and military elite. Russia's military elite, led by Chief-of-Staff General Mikhail Alexeev, believed that in order to restore military discipline and ensure the survival of the empire, the Tsar had to abdicate from the throne. Alexeev sent a telegram to Nicholas advising him to abdicate. Grand Duke Nikolai Nikolaevich, the Tsar's uncle who was a respected military commander, also sent a telegram to his nephew advising him to abdicate. Thus, the Tsar lost the support of the military elite as well as the rank-and-file. Nevertheless, encouraged by letters from his wife which suggested that there was nothing to worry about, the Tsar ignored all requests to abdicate and remained at headquarters, relying on the police, and if necessary, his loyal Guard regiments.

On 27 February, Nicholas received news that most of his Guards regiments had joined the masses on the streets of Petrograd. The Volynsky Life Guard Regiment was the first to mutiny, and this triggered the mutiny of the remaining guards garrisoned in the capital. A particularly bitter blow to the Tsar was the fact that the Preobrazhensky Regiment—the most prestigious military unit in the army, originally created by Peter the Great—had joined the demonstrations against the Tsar. As a result of the mutiny, the revolutionaries were now armed. Over 40,000 rifles fell into the hands of the workers as they hunted down the police. The defection of most of his army deprived the Tsar of his final bastion of loyalty. The mutinies did not only serve to weaken the war effort but also posed a mortal threat to the survival of the Romanov dynasty. Nicholas finally realized the danger to his rule and decided he had to return to his capital to restore order. At five in the morning on 28

February, he left General Headquarters and headed to Petrograd on his royal train.

While returning to the capital, the imperial train was intercepted and could go no further, as the railroads leading to the capital were occupied by revolutionaries. The railroad workers were among the most enthusiastic supporters of the revolution. Their route blocked, the royal train was forced to divert to the ancient city of Pskov, arriving on the evening of 1 March. Meanwhile, units at the Alexander Palace were abandoning the Tsar and leaving for Petrograd to join the demonstrations. At the train station in Pskov, the Tsar was met by General Nikolai Ruzsky and monarchist Duma deputies Alexander Guchkov and Vasily Shulgin, who presented Nicholas with an abdication manifesto. Ruzsky spoke forcefully in the presence of the Tsar, blaming him for the military and political failures and warning him that if he were to refuse to sign, his life would be in danger. Reluctantly, Nicholas signed the abdication manifesto that had been prepared for him.

At 3:00 the following afternoon, after a sleepless night, Nicholas II requested a change to his abdication manifesto. Tsarevich Alexei was not yet thirteen and was unlikely to live beyond his teens due to his incurable illness. He would also be succeeding to the throne at a politically dangerous juncture. Nicholas was also fully aware that his son would be in no position to wield any effective political power and defend the interests of the imperial court. For these reasons, Nicholas decided to abdicate on behalf of his son for the sake of the young Tsarevich, but he passed the throne to his younger brother, Grand Duke Mikhail Alexandrovich. It was this version of the abdication manifesto that was subsequently made public.

Nicholas's decision to pass the throne to Grand Duke Mikhail was completely unexpected. The men who had persuaded the Tsar to abdicate anticipated that Tsarevich Alexei, as the lawful heir to the throne, would assume the offices of emperor and tsar and the monarchy would remain in place. The Tsar's decision to abdicate on behalf of his son was probably illegal. The Law of Succession which governed the dynastic succession of the Romanovs since 1797 stipulated that the Tsar would be succeeded by his eldest son and did not allow the monarch to intervene in the choice of a successor, and had been the practice instituted by Peter the Great. If the Tsar wished to change the succession—as he had considered doing so before Alexei's birth—he would have to repeal the law and introduce a new one. The situation was further complicated by the fact that Nicholas had previously excluded Mikhail from the succession due to his morganatic marriage—and scandalous relationship—with Natalia Brasova. Nevertheless, the Tsar's wish was granted while he still exercised autocratic power.

News of the Tsar's decision to transfer the throne to his brother confounded the expectations of the remaining defenders of the monarchy in Petrograd. They reckoned a young Tsar Alexei would not be able to exercise effective political power until he reached adulthood, which was by no means guaranteed. During this period, political power would be exercised by representative bodies such as the Duma rather than the imperial court. Indeed, twelve Duma deputies had already formed a Provisional Committee that would take care of government business. This would give the government, which enjoyed public confidence, the opportunity to restore order in Petrograd and continue the war. Instead, the prospect of Tsar Mikhail at the helm meant that the court would continue to exercise its authority, even under a constitutional monarchy. Consequently, the Duma moved to prevent Mikhail from assuming the throne.

When Mikhail Alexandrovich first heard the news that he was to inherit the throne, he was excited by the prospect. In discussions with Pavel Milyukov and Alexander Kerensky, both senior Duma politicians, the Grand Duke was enthusiastic about being a constitutional monarch like a British king—enjoying all the pomp and circumstance of imperial office without the burden of discharging the functions of government. Kerensky persuaded the Grand Duke that since the situation in Petrograd was still unstable, by assuming the throne Mikhail would be placing himself in danger.

Accordingly, on 3 March the Grand Duke released a statement in which he declared that he would only accept the throne if it was offered to him by the Constituent Assembly, a representative body which would be summoned later in the year to decide on future constitutional matters.

Despite the Grand Duke's suggestion that he might one day assume the throne, Petrograd seemed ready to reject the Romanovs completely. The Romanov dynasty, which had celebrated its tercentennial with much pomp and circumstance in 1913, was no more. Imperial symbols such as the double-headed eagle and the Tsarist tricolor flag were torn down from buildings on Nevsky Prospekt, the main thoroughfare of the Russian capital. They were replaced by a sea of red flags, while everyone in the capital was obliged to wear red clothing in public lest they be attacked for being a counterrevolutionary. Even Grand Duke Kirill, Nicholas II's cousin, tied a red handkerchief to his rifle in an effort to maintain military discipline in the regiment he commanded. The national anthem *God Save the Tsar* was replaced—unofficially—with the 18th-century religious hymn *How Great is Our Lord in Zion*. In the streets, revolutionaries sang the *Internationale* and the *Workers' Marseillaise*, a Russian version of the French national anthem with more radical lyrics. On 9 March, Nicholas II—now merely 'Colonel Nicholas Romanov'—and his family were placed under house arrest at the Alexander Palace. In Petrograd, however, it was as if the Romanovs were already long gone.

Chapter 3 – Dual Power

Although the Tsar did not abdicate until the beginning of March, the series of demonstrations that toppled the Romanov regime came to be known as the February Revolution. Following the Tsar's abdication, a Provisional Government was formed by leading Duma politicians. The body met at the Tauride Palace in Petrograd's Liteiny Prospekt, where the Duma previously met. On 3 March, the Provisional Government published an official announcement in which it announced that it was taking over the duties of the Tsarist government. The Provisional Government was self-declared and was not elected. The ten-man body was designed to manage day-to-day affairs of governments while preparing for elections to the Constituent Assembly later in the year.

The initial composition of the Provisional Government heavily favored liberal political parties. The liberals favored parliamentary government based on British and American models. They actively encouraged capitalism and business activity and many liberals remained monarchists, albeit favoring a monarchy that enjoyed far less political power. The Prime Minister was Prince Georgy Lvov, an aristocrat whose lineage stretched even further than the Romanovs. Lvov had been chairman of the Union of Zemstvos during the war, a body created to coordinate the activities of the elected village councils across the country which provided material assistance to the war effort in the form of supplies and military hospitals. A physically imposing figure with a long beard, Lvov was not affiliated to a political party and was rarely in the public eye.

Most of Lvov's ministers were Kadets—officially known as the Constitutional Democratic Party. The Kadets were formed following a split in the Russian liberal movement in 1905 after Nicholas II issued the October Manifesto that established the Duma. Unlike the Octobrist Party, which was satisfied by the concessions offered by the Tsar, the Kadets envisaged the Duma as a platform by which it would call for more radical political reforms, including universal civil rights, the ending of censorship, the legalization of trade unions, and the right to free education. The Kadets were led by the historian Pavel Milyukov, who became Foreign Minister in the new government.

Another prominent member of the Provisional Government was Minister of War Alexander Guchkov, the leader of the Octobrist Party. The Octobrist Party—or the Union of 17 October—was established in 1905 to support Nicholas II after he promulgated the October Manifesto. The Octobrist Party was well represented in the Third Duma between 1906 and 1910 and Guchkov and his party supported the political program of Prime Minister Pyotr Stolypin. Appointed Chairman of the Central War Industry Committee in 1915, Guchkov played a significant contribution to the effort to ensure the army was well supplied with arms and ammunition. While the Octobrists were monarchists and supported Romanov rule after 1905, over the course of the war Guchkov came to the conclusion that Nicholas had to be removed. He was one of the Duma deputies who met the Tsar in Pskov and persuaded him to abdicate.

Although the Provisional Government was soon recognized as the legitimate government in Russia by its British and French allies, its political power was limited. It was forced to compete for political power with the Petrograd Soviet, which met in the opposite wing of the Tauride Palace. While the Provisional Government represented the liberals, the Petrograd Soviet of Workers', Soldiers' and Sailors'

Deputies represented the interests of the city's working class who were responsible for the strikes and disturbances that signaled the loss of confidence in the Tsarist regime. The body also included representatives from the army and the navy who joined the revolution. In fact, most of the deputies were soldiers. The presence of the army rank-and-file in the Petrograd Soviet meant that Order No. 1, issued on 1 March, proclaimed that the army and navy would only carry out orders from the government with approval from the Soviet. This proved a significant limitation to the powers of the Provisional Government, which sought to keep Russia in the First World War.

The Petrograd Soviet was dominated by two parties, the Socialist Revolutionaries (SRs), and the Mensheviks. Led by Viktor Chernov, the SRs inherited the ideology of the Populist movement, which espoused a form of agrarian socialism based on the Russian peasant commune. This meant that the SRs were primarily Slavophiles who supported Russian traditions and turned away from foreign ideas such as Marxism. Although the party did attempt to appeal to workers by adopting some Marxist ideas, the party's base remained in the Russian countryside. Nevertheless, it managed to win the support of a significant proportion of the Petrograd proletariat. The radical wing of the party, the Left SRs, carried out a series of high profile political assassinations at the beginning of the 20th century. The most significant victims were Interior Minister Vyacheslav von Plehve in 1904 and Grand Duke Sergei (Nicholas II's uncle) in 1905.

The leadership of the Petrograd Soviet was dominated by the Mensheviks, who were not officially a political party, but rather a fraction of the Russian Social Democratic Party (RSDP, or SDs), which was inspired by Marxist policies and aspired to the support of the Russian working class. The SDs split into two major factions in 1903, when senior leaders Vladimir Lenin and Julius Martov fell out over questions of party strategy and organization. Lenin argued that the Russian proletariat was ready to take power on behalf of the people, and the party should consist of professional revolutionaries acting as the "vanguard of the proletariat." Martov was more moderate and believed the party should grow a large member base and wait until Russia was further industrialized before seeking to overthrow the establishment. Lenin forced a vote in the party's central committee which he won. He therefore called his faction the Bolsheviks or Majoritarians, while Martov's supporters were known as Mensheviks, or Minoritarians. Despite this distinction, until 1917 the Mensheviks enjoyed far higher levels of support among the Russian working class than the Bolsheviks. While the Mensheviks participated in parliamentary politics, the Bolsheviks refused to participate. Lenin's ideas were too radical and his influence was limited. Nikolai Chkeidze, the first Chairman of the Petrograd Soviet, was an influential Georgian Menshevik.

The Provisional Government and the Petrograd Soviet depended on each other's support to exercise political power, a state of affairs described as 'dual power.' It may be said that while the Provisional Government enjoyed authority without power, the Petrograd Soviet enjoyed power without authority. Although the two bodies represented different class interests, inspired by the euphoria of the February Revolution both bodies worked together for a six-week period later called the 'honeymoon of the revolution.' Furthermore, the SRs, and especially the Mensheviks, believed that Russia required a lengthy period of bourgeois capitalism before the conditions were ripe for socialism. During this period of frantic activity, the Provisional Government, supported and encouraged by the Petrograd Soviet, introduced a series of liberal reforms dismantling the autocratic state of the tsars. These included an end to censorship, guaranteed civil rights and freedoms, and the release of political prisoners. In the army, ranks were abolished and epaulets removed from uniforms. Lenin, returning to Russia from exile in Switzerland, described Russia as "the freest country in the world."

The cooperation between the two bodies was facilitated by Alexander Kerensky, who uniquely held positions of responsibility in both organizations. A member of the Trudovik Party, which was closely aligned with the Socialist-Revolutionaries, Kerensky was the only socialist minister in the Provisional Government, serving as Minister of Justice. At the same time, he was also Vice Chair of the Petrograd Soviet and was a well-respected socialist revolutionary. Owing to these commitments, Kerensky was often seen running from one end of the Tauride Palace to the other in order to mediate and transmit messages between the two organizations. When Kerensky appeared in meetings of the Provisional Government, he would wear a suit and tie like his fellow ministers. As he made his way to the Soviet, he would remove his tie and wear a worker's cap. It is likely that he had to perform this routine several times a day, especially when contentious issues were being debated. For this reason alone, Kerensky was most likely the hardest working politician in Petrograd during the immediate aftermath of the revolution.

The honeymoon of the revolution came to an abrupt end in mid-April when the War Aims Crisis broke out. While Russia remained a participant in the First World War alongside Britain and France, the nature of her participation was questioned, especially in the Petrograd Soviet. Some deputies believed that Russia should end the war as soon as possible regardless of territorial losses, since the international proletariat would invariably destroy the German and Austrian empires in due course. The majority of deputies were more realistic and adopted a policy of 'revolutionary defencism.' Under this policy, the Russian army would continue fighting to defend territory which had belonged to the Russian Empire but would not seek to occupy and annex territory at the expense of its enemies. Matters came to a head on 18 April when a telegram sent by Foreign Minister Pavel Milyukov to the Allies was leaked to the press. Milyukov stated that Russia would not only remain an active participant in the war but underlined that in the event of victory, the Allies would remain obliged to honor their guarantee of transferring Constantinople and the Turkish Straits to Russian control. This was part of an agreement the Allies had made with Tsar Nicholas II in 1915.

The War Aims Crisis threatened the integrity of the Provisional Government. Milyukov's telegram sparked a demonstration on the streets of the capital, and the Petrograd Soviet made it clear that it did not support the Provisional Government's war aims. On 24 April, Milyukov realized his position was untenable and resigned from his post. The Ukrainian industrialist Mikhail Tereshchenko replaced him. Guchkov, who supported Milyukov on the issue, also left his post as War Minister. Alexander Kerensky, whose political profile continued to rise, was appointed to the office of War Minister. In response to the crisis, Lvov offered ministerial positions to five other moderate socialists representing the Mensheviks and the SRs. Viktor Chernov, the leader of the SRs, became Minister of Agriculture. Three new positions were created to reflect the political program of the socialist parties: Minister of Labor, Minister of Food, Minister of Post and Telegraph.

It might be expected that the increased presence of socialist ministers in the Provisional Government would have facilitated co-operation between the Provisional Government and the Petrograd Soviet. In fact, after April 1917 relations between the two organizations were increasingly marked by conflict and suspicion rather than co-operation. Invited into government, the socialist ministers came to appreciate the scale of Russia's military and economic difficulties but lacked the means and the will to take decisive action. The Provisional Government deferred action on important issues such as land redistribution, arguing that it was a matter for the Constituent Assembly. Lack of action on key issues resulted in a deterioration of the military and economic situation and contributed to the government losing support.

Furthermore, the economic problems that afflicted Russia impacted the whole country rather than Petrograd itself. Neither the Provisional Government nor the Petrograd Soviet was able to exercise power beyond Petrograd and its outskirts. British historian Orlando Figes argues that central authority had broken down in February. Although the Petrograd Soviet sought to co-ordinate the actions of city and regional soviets throughout the country, their efforts met with mixed success since the political composition of local soviets varied significantly. Thus, political power was concentrated at the level of city and region rather than in the capital. The Provisional Government would also face difficulties from Lenin's Bolsheviks, which gained popularity over the course of the year due to its uncompromising stance.

Chapter 4 – Return from exile

The February Revolution and the Tsar's abdication had taken Lenin by surprise. In late 1916, in an address to international socialists in Switzerland, he said that he did not expect to see a revolution in Russia during his lifetime. In exile, Lenin found it difficult to receive accurate information about the situation in Russia. It is likely that he received news about Russia from the international press, which suggested that Russia's military fortunes were improving. Even when he received news of the Tsar's abdication, he was skeptical. False rumors were easily spread during the war for propaganda purposes. When Lenin became convinced that the news was genuine, he made plans for an immediate return to Russia. He had waited for twenty years for the outbreak of revolution in Russia, and when it came to pass he was absent. He was determined to return and put his plans into action.

Vladimir Ilyich Ulyanov was not a born revolutionary. His father Ilya was a school inspector in Simbirsk province, a position of responsibility which made him a hereditary noble. The young Vladimir seemed destined for a career in the imperial bureaucracy. This idyllic childhood was shattered in 1886 when his older brother, Alexander Ulyanov, a student at St Petersburg University, was hanged after participating in a plot to kill Tsar Alexander III. This traumatic event encouraged Vladimir to take a greater interest in revolutionary politics. He was expelled from Kazan University for participating in revolutionary activities, although he was eventually allowed to take his exams in St Petersburg. This did not deter him from further political activity, and he was soon introduced to the works of Karl Marx.

In the 1890s, Vladimir Ulyanov began to read the works of Russian Marxist Georgy Plekhanov. He agreed with Plekhanov's idea that Russia was transitioning from feudalism to capitalism, consequently the Russian working class would act as the agent for socialist revolution. This was the founding principle of the Russian Marxist Party in 1898, which was renamed the Russian Social Democratic Labour Party in 1900. Ulyanov founded the radical newspaper *Iskra* which served as the party's official newspaper. In 1901, he began to adopt the pseudonym N. Lenin, though the reason behind his choice is unclear. In 1902 he published *What is to be Done?*, his first major theoretical work. The treatise, which shared a title with Nikolay Chernyshevsky's revolutionary novel from 1863, confronted elements among the Social Democrats who were in favor of co-operating with bourgeois elements as an intermediary step to full socialism.

Lenin's publication sparked an intense theoretical debate within the Russian Social Democratic Party. Using the examples of Britain and Germany, Marx had argued that historical laws dictated that society should move from feudalism to bourgeois capitalism, and only then onto socialism and finally communism. The transition from capitalism to socialism could only begin once the capitalist stage managed to accumulate enough wealth. Russian society only began to shift from feudalism to capitalism at the end of the nineteenth century. Lenin's opponents therefore argued, according to Marx's theory, that Russian capitalism should be allowed to develop for a couple of generations before the time was ripe for a challenge to the new order. Workers could challenge factory owners by demanding higher wages and better working conditions but should not seek to overthrow the capitalist order. Lenin put forward an alternate theory in which he argued that bourgeois capitalism was at its weakest precisely when it was in its early stages. If workers were to form trade unions and demand better working conditions, in an effort to avoid revolution the capitalists may be encouraged to conciliate with union leaders and develop friendlier relations, albeit ones that continued to exploit the workers. This had been happening in Germany and the United Kingdom, where conservative governments were introducing welfare reforms and sanctioning the establishment of trade unions. Lenin believed that the longer this happened, the more difficult it would be to encourage the working classes to overthrow the bourgeois order.

As described in the previous chapter, the RSDLP split into two major factions in 1903. As leader of the Bolsheviks, Lenin sought to create a professional revolutionary organization dedicated to overthrowing the Tsarist autocracy, applying the principles he had set out in *What is to be Done?* In order to maintain party discipline, Lenin rejected pluralism within the party, maintaining a tight grip on the decision-making process within the party. The Bolsheviks rejected parliamentary democracy and refused to participate in the elections to the Imperial Duma in April 1906. Although the Bolsheviks did participate in the elections to the Second Duma in July, their performance was modest in comparison to the Socialist Revolutionaries and the Mensheviks. Lenin's uncompromising politics made himself and leading Bolsheviks targets for the Tsarist secret police. As a result, Lenin and his fellow Bolsheviks spent much of the early twentieth century avoiding the Russian authorities and conducting his revolutionary activities in exile in a number of cities in western and central Europe, including London, Geneva, Paris, and Krakow.

Despite Lenin's conception that the Bolsheviks would serve as the vanguard of the revolution, his party played a minimal role in the events in February that led to Nicholas II's abdication. This was not altogether surprising, since most of the Bolshevik leaders were in internal or external exile. The amnesty for political prisoners ensured that exiled Bolsheviks could freely return to Russia. While Bolsheviks like Stalin who were exiled in Siberia found it relatively straightforward to return to Petrograd, Lenin found himself in a difficult position by being in Switzerland. In order to return to Russia by the most direct route, he would have to travel across Germany, which was still enemy territory for a man who remained a Russian citizen, no matter how many times he had fallen foul of the authorities under Tsarist rule. Fortunately, the German authorities decided to let him do just that.

The German Empire, born out of Prussian conservatism, was no friend of revolutionaries like Lenin. Nevertheless, the German government realized that Lenin could further destabilize the Russian war effort, allowing German armies to make further conquests, or alternatively force an advantageous peace treaty for Germany. The German authorities allowed Lenin to travel across the empire in a sealed train. In fact, Lenin and his fellow revolutionaries were given a single carriage, and other passengers could freely board the train's other carriages. Lenin insisted the carriage be granted "extra-territorial status" to "seal" it from contact with Germans. This included a chalk line dividing the Russian exiles' territory from the German territory of the military guards on board.

Lenin and his fellow exiles, all of them revolutionaries including his wife, Nadezhda Krupskaya, had boarded the train in Zurich, crossed Germany, traveled the Baltic Sea by ferry and ridden 17 hours by rail from Stockholm 700 miles north to Haparanda. They hired horse-drawn sleds to head across the frozen river to Finland. "I remember that it was night," Grigory Zinoviev, one of the exiles traveling with Lenin, would write in a memoir. "There was a long thin ribbon of sledges. On each sledge were two people. Tension as [we] approached the Finnish border reached its maximum....Vladimir Ilyich was outwardly calm." Eight days later, he would reach Petrograd. Lenin did not fail to make use of the time he spent on the train back to Russia. He worked frantically on a political program for the Bolsheviks to adopt.

Lenin condemned the Provisional Government as bourgeois and urged unconditional opposition to it, as "the utter falsity of all its promises should be made clear." He condemned World War I as a "predatory imperialist war" and the "revolutionary defencism" of foreign social democrat parties. He supported a policy of revolutionary defeatism, arguing that Russia should end the war as quickly as possible. He asserted that the power must be placed in the hand of the proletariat and the poorest section of peasants. The slogan 'Peace, Land, and Bread' was an indication of Lenin's political priorities. He understood that most people wanted an end to a war from which they had nothing to gain. He was also aware of the crippling food shortages in the capital and the necessity to ensure that Petrograd workers could afford food. Lenin was also keen to redistribute aristocratic land among peasants in the Russian country side. Above all, Lenin hoped to overthrow the Provisional Government and bring the means of economic production under the control of the Soviets of Workers' Deputies. To encapsulate this idea, he promoted the slogan 'All Power to the Soviets.'

On 3 April, Lenin arrived at Petrograd's Finland station where he was enthusiastically welcomed by cheering crowds. No sooner had he arrived in Russia, Lenin began to mobilize support for his policies. On 4 April, Lenin published the April Theses—the program which he developed on the train—and sought to convince fellow party members to adopt his line. The April Theses came as a surprise to most of the Bolshevik leadership. Senior leaders, including Lev Kamenev and Grigory Zinoviev, felt that Lenin had gone mad and the years he spent in foreign exile made him lose all sense of perspective in terms of the material situation in Russia. While most Bolsheviks were not keen on the Provisional Government, they aimed for greater representation in the Petrograd Soviet intending eventually to form a coalition government with the SRs and Mensheviks.

Lenin was soon to find a useful ally in his effort to convince his fellow Bolsheviks. Like Lenin, Leon Trotsky was in exile when the February Revolution broke out. Living in New York, Trotsky had a longer and no less arduous journey to make in order to return to Russia. He left New York on 14 March 1917, aboard the SS Kristianiafjord. The neutral Norwegian vessel was intercepted by British naval officials in Canada at Halifax, Nova Scotia, and Trotsky was detained for a month at Amherst Internment Camp in Nova Scotia. During this period, he established warm relationships with his fellow inmates and won respect among them for his political perspectives. Meanwhile the Provisional Government's Foreign Minister Pavel Milyukov, pressured by the Petrograd Soviet, reluctantly demanded from Russia's British allies that Trotsky be released as a Russian citizen, which was successful on 16 April 1917. He reached Russia on 4 May, and after his return, Trotsky substantially agreed with the Bolshevik position, but did not join them right away.

A collaborator of Lenin's during the early days of the RSDLP, Trotsky did not identify with either of the main factions of the party, though more often than not he sided with the Mensheviks. Once the February Revolution had broken out, Trotsky was on the same page as Lenin. He took care not to break completely with the Mensheviks, but over the course of 1917 he moved ever closer to Lenin's position. After his arrival in Russia, Trotsky was a very useful ally for Lenin as the latter tirelessly campaigned to have the April Theses adopted as party policy. Trotsky was a talented and passionate public speaker, and his rhetorical skills certainly surpassed those of Lenin. He was also an experienced revolutionary, having served as briefly as President of the Petrograd Soviet during its first incarnation in 1905. Trotsky soon established himself as a senior member of the Bolshevik party leadership, second only to Lenin himself.

The uncompromising position held by Lenin, Trotsky, and eventually the Bolsheviks as a whole, soon paid dividends. The Provisional Government continued to lose support due to its inability to address the key economic issues that afflicted Petrograd. The presence of Menshevik and SR ministers in the Provisional Government contributed to a corresponding decline in popularity for their respective parties. As the largest party to demonstrate open opposition to the government, the Bolsheviks became increasingly popular. When the February Revolution broke out there were only 2,000 members of the Bolshevik Party in Petrograd. By April this number increased to 16,000. By the beginning of July, the party could count on the support of 200,000 members in the capital.

Chapter 5 – The July Days

Since the February Revolution, the Russian army in the front line was largely reduced to fighting defensive actions. In mid-June, War Minister Alexander Kerensky gave orders for an offensive by General Brusilov's army in Galicia, largely following the path laid out by the Brusilov Offensive the previous year. Kerensky hoped that a successful offensive would enable the Provisional Government to gain credibility both in the eyes of the Allies and within Russia itself. Kerensky hoped to show the world that the 'most democratic army in the world' could defeat the Austrians and Germans. This belief was not completely unjustified. Kerensky hoped to emulate the example of the French Revolutionary armies who were able to defeat *ancien regime* armies, motivated by the élan associated with new-found identity and citizenship. Kerensky hoped that the soldiers would be inspired to defend the gains of the revolution. In this he was supported by All-Russian Soviet of Workers' and Soldiers' Deputies, the umbrella body for soviets across the country.

Kerensky's expectations did not come to pass. While the Russian army initially managed to surprise the Austrians, it soon ran out of steam. By the time the German-Austrian army was able to launch a counter-attack, the Russian forces lost cohesion and broke ranks. The lack of military hierarchy and discipline prevented the Russian army from retreating in an orderly fashion. Unlike the French

Revolutionary Wars, the Russian army had already been fighting the First World War for three exhausting years. The French Revolutionary armies carried battlefields on the point their bayonets. The developments in projectile technology over the course of a century made bayonet charges less effective in the First World War. Consequently, this most democratic of all armies was cut down by enemy fire, and those that survived fled the ranks. Bereft of morale and discipline, the Russian army sustained casualties amounting to 60,000 men. This was twice the number of the casualties suffered by the Austro-German army.

As news of the failure of the Kerensky Offensive filtered through to Petrograd and the Provisional Government called up reinforcements from the Petrograd garrison, the Petrograd Soviet refused to sanction Kerensky's orders and the soldiers refused to go to the front. On 3 July, a crowd of 70,000 people, including mutinous soldiers, flocked to the streets of Petrograd staging demonstrations. The demonstrations received active support from disillusioned soldiers on the front line. In a letter addressed to the Petrograd Soviet, a junior NCO named Yurchenko expresses his regret that the war has to continue with the shedding of innocent blood: "Is the German really trying to infringe on our freedom? No, on the contrary, this is just something made up by the bourgeois ministers, who tell us that we have to strengthen freedom, but at the same time they're killing people in this offensive of theirs and what can come of that?"

The scenes were reminiscent of those which caused the downfall of the Romanovs, and the Provisional Government appeared to be hanging by a thread. The Bolsheviks, who had been eagerly anticipating the overthrow of the Provisional Government, seemed destined to take power at any moment. For much of his life, and indeed for much of 1917, Lenin sought to convince everyone around him that the Bolsheviks had to take power immediately. Once again, however, events in the streets of Petrograd had taken Lenin by surprise, since he was on vacation in Finland when the demonstrations started. Upon his return on 4 July, 20,000 armed sailors from Kronstadt gathered outside Bolshevik Party Headquarters, established in the premises of the mansion of ballerina Matilda Kshesinskaya, Nicholas II's former mistress. They clamored for Lenin to make an appearance, expecting him to welcome them enthusiastically and give them instructions to arrest both the Provisional Government and the Petrograd Soviet. Instead, Lenin did not appear for a long time, and once he did he delivered brief and vague remarks in which he applauded their enthusiasm but refused to sanction the demonstrations and failed to give clear orders. On the following day, an official notice was published in the Bolshevik newspaper *Pravda* which called for the masses to disperse.

Why did Lenin refuse to support the masses during the July Days when it appeared that the Bolshevik Party itself had stirred them up in the first place? Some historians argue that the Bolshevik leadership encouraged the demonstrations in an effort to establish their level of support without the intention of taking power. Others argue that the July Days came as a surprise to Lenin. He considered the protestors to be an unruly mob, one which could easily turn against him. At any rate, this was a far cry from the party of disciplined professional revolutionaries whom he sought to create. There were good reasons for Lenin to avoid taking action in July. Although the party was becoming more popular by the day, the Bolsheviks did not have sufficient support among the Petrograd proletariat, not to speak of the rest of the country. Even if the Bolsheviks were to gain control in the capital, they may still face resistance from the rest of the country. Furthermore, it would be incongruous for the Bolsheviks to seize power in the name of the soviets against the wishes of the Petrograd Soviet.

After Lenin's refusal to lead them, the masses decided to take their complaints to the Petrograd Soviet. A crowd of 50,000 gathered outside the Tauride Palace, criticizing the SR and Menshevik ministers who had joined the Provisional Government. The protesters demanded to speak to the Soviet leadership and hear their explanations for refusing to take power. The SR leader and Minister of Agriculture Viktor Chernov appeared and attempted to calm the masses by justifying the Petrograd Soviet's position to the crowd of soldiers, workers, and sailors. Instead of placating the crowd, the demonstrators steadily grew more hostile, and Chernov was seized by a group of particularly zealous protestors. He was only released following the timely intervention of Trotsky, who fought his way through the crowd and requested they let go of the SR leader who had been bundled into a car. Had the Bolsheviks actively sought to overthrow the regime, there would have been no better opportunity to exploit the confusion and storm the Tauride Palace.

Although half a million people may have been involved in the July demonstrations, they soon dispersed once they recognized that they would not receive any support from either the Petrograd Soviet or the Bolshevik leadership. This gave the Provisional Government the opportunity it needed to reassert control. By 7 July, the expression of anger from the Petrograd masses had dissipated, with minimal casualties. But the July Days did lay bare the existential threat posed by the workers and soldiers both to the Russian bourgeoisie and to the government itself. Even if the leadership did not throw its weight behind the demonstrations, Bolshevik activists were actively involved in encouraging the soldiers of the Petrograd garrison to mutiny. The Provisional Government therefore launched a counter-revolutionary campaign which forced the Bolshevik Party into clandestine activity once again as the responsibility for the uprising was laid squarely at the feet of Lenin and the Bolsheviks, both by the Provisional Government and moderate elements in the Soviet.

As part of the effort to prevent the July Days from happening again, the Provisional Government, with support from the Petrograd Soviet, moved to suppress the Bolshevik leadership. The government ordered the arrest of Lenin and other prominent Bolsheviks, raiding their offices, shutting down *Pravda*, and publicly alleging that Lenin was a German *agent provocateur* who had received money and instructions from the German government to overthrow the Provisional Government and take Russia out of the war. The fact that

Lenin received financial assistance from the German government while returning to Russia seemed to reflect this, though this did not necessarily mean that he was receiving instructions from Berlin. Lenin first evaded arrest by hiding in many safe houses in Petrograd. Eventually, fearing an attempt on his life, he fled to the small settlement of Razliv in disguise with fellow Bolshevik Grigory Zinoviev. There, Lenin began work on the book that would become *The State and Revolution*, an exposition on how he believed the socialist state would develop after the proletariat revolution and how from then on the state would gradually wither away, leaving a pure communist society as Marx had envisaged. The book describes the role of the State in society, the necessity of proletarian revolution, and the theoretic inadequacies of social democracy—espoused by the Mensheviks—in achieving revolution to establish the dictatorship of the proletariat. At first, he urged for a Bolshevik-led insurrection to topple the government, but the idea was rejected. Hence, Lenin headed to Finland and arrived at Helsinki on 10 August, where he hid away in safe houses belonging to Bolshevik sympathizers. Other Bolshevik leaders were not as fortunate. Trotsky, Kamenev, and Lunacharsky were arrested and all remained in prison until Kerensky released them in late August.

Much of the repressive actions taken against the Bolshevik leaders were not carried out by the liberal prime minister Georgy Lvov but the socialist Alexander Kerensky. The July Days had plunged the Provisional Government into crisis. Several liberal ministers resigned from the government following a decision by the government to recognize the establishment of an independent Ukrainian government. The Mensheviks and SRs, who could have taken power through the Petrograd Soviet, decided instead to seek to form a new coalition with liberals in the Provisional Government. On 6 July, Alexander Kerensky returned to Petrograd after efforts to rally the demoralized troops at the front, ensuring that the offensive was not a complete disaster. He was welcomed back as a national hero and regarded as the only person who could reunite the country. On 8 July, Lvov resigned as Prime Minister, much to his own relief.

Lvov recognized that he lacked the will to eliminate the Petrograd Soviet, which he saw as the only way to save the country. Kerensky's appointment to the highest office marked the zenith of the cult of Kerensky, who was regarded by the cultural intelligentsia, including theater directors Stanislavsky and Nemirovich-Danchenko, as the embodiment of the Russian national ideal. It is said that Kerensky was drunk on the enthusiastic support he enjoyed, and began to regard himself as a Russian Napoleon Bonaparte, the man who would end the excesses of the revolution while preserving its gains. Critics claimed that he changed his signature so that 'Alexander K.' now resembled 'Alexander IV.'

Kerensky wished to establish the central government as a strong authority, reversing some of the liberal measures introduced in the euphoric days and weeks following the February Revolution. In response to the demonstrations of the July Days, he began enacting measures to impose discipline in Petrograd to prevent the resumption of civil disorder. Street processions in Petrograd were banned and any publication that provoked disorder was forbidden as a part of an effort to maintain civil order in the city. The government also held a public funeral for Cossack soldiers who were killed by July Day participants on 15 July. On 18 July, Kerensky moved the new government ministers into the Winter Palace and ordered the Soviet to move from the Tauride Palace to the Smolny Institute down the road. This decision was of great symbolic importance. By returning the seat of government to the Winter Palace in the heart of Petrograd, Kerensky hoped to establish a form of continuity with the Tsarist regime which had ruled Russia for many centuries. The Smolny Institute, on the other hand, had served as a finishing school for aristocratic daughters and was located far from the city center. The two parties which together held dual power now operated from separate premises. Over the course of 1917, the Provisional Government and the Petrograd Soviet drifted away from each other politically. In July, they were moved apart physically.

Chapter 6 – The abortive coup

The July Days and the ministerial crisis left the Provisional Government standing on a precipice. Kerensky moved further away from his former colleagues in the Petrograd Soviet in an effort to conciliate liberals and conservatives who favored the re-imposition of political order. A week after taking office, Kerensky dismissed Brusilov and appointed the hardline General Lavr Kornilov as commander-in-chief, giving him a mandate to restore military discipline in the army. This would not only serve to improve Russia's fortunes in the war but also ensure that soldiers could be relied on to maintain order in the capital. Kornilov's appointment was supported by Russia's industrial and business elite, who feared the consequences of a socialist government under the Bolsheviks. Despite having been a socialist firebrand himself, Kerensky recognized the necessity of imposing order and discipline in Petrograd to ensure that his government could carry out its day-to-day duties effectively.

A military officer with Siberian Cossack origins, Kornilov was a rare exception among Russia's military elite, most of whom could boast of distinguished aristocratic lineages. He spent much of his military career serving in Central and Eastern Asia. During the First World War, he was taken into Austrian captivity in 1915 but managed to escape the following year, returning to Russia on foot. By the time of the February Revolution, he was placed in command of the

Petrograd Military District and gave orders to keep Nicholas II and his family under house arrest. This suggests that he was sympathetic to the revolution, at least to the liberal bourgeois Provisional Government. During the summer offensive of 1917, Kornilov's men achieved the most success, his cavalry units overcoming Austrian defenses while most Russian infantry units had already been stopped in their tracks. Kornilov was therefore one of few officers to emerge from the June offensive with an enhanced reputation. Kerensky had already appointed him to command the Southwestern Front. These factors made him an obvious choice as Brusilov's replacement for the supreme command.

In order to fulfil his mandate, Kornilov proposed a series of reforms to maintain order and discipline in both military and civilian life. These ranged from the abolition of the soldiers' committees established in accordance with the Petrograd Soviet's Order No. 1 to the restoration of the death penalty for civilians and the imposition of martial law throughout the country. In effect, Kornilov was seeking to establish a military dictatorship. Kornilov argued that this was a necessary step to ensure order and tranquility in the streets of Petrograd, protecting the Provisional Government from any attempts to overthrow it. This placed the Prime Minister in a dilemma and Kerensky was unenthusiastic about Kornilov's plans. Kerensky appreciated Kornilov's intention to restore military control but felt uneasy about the prospect of Kornilov effectively acting as military dictator and challenging his own authority as head of the civil government. Even if he had no immediate intentions to do so, Kornilov could easily be in a position to remove Kerensky from the office of Prime Minister. For these reasons, the Prime Minister was reluctant to approve his commander-in-chief's radical reform program.

On 25 August, Kornilov gave orders for a corps under the command of General Alexander Krymov to enter Petrograd with instructions to suppress the Petrograd Soviet. It is unclear why Kornilov gave this order. It is possible that Kornilov heard rumors of a Bolshevik coup planned for the end of August and ordered Krymov to strengthen the defense of the capital. More likely, Kornilov anticipated that his military reforms would be announced by the government, which would inevitably result in the outbreak of protests. Under this pretext, Krymov could use his men to suppress the Petrograd Soviet. This was a trigger for a political crisis subsequently known as the Kornilov Affair. While Kornilov had issued his orders in an effort to save the Provisional Government, Kerensky began to fear that he was intent on overthrowing it. Relations between the two men were increasingly strained. Kerensky believed that Kornilov had Napoleonic ambitions and was seeking to replace him, while Kornilov considered Kerensky a weak leader who was under the control of the Petrograd Soviet and whose indecisive leadership would inevitably deliver a Bolshevik revolution. The two men clashed publicly at a State Conference in Moscow held on 12-14 August, summoned by Kerensky in an effort to rally the country behind him. Kerensky spoke of the need to restore order with 'blood and iron.' The Prime Minister was followed by his supreme commander, who directly provoked the former by announcing that he had presented Kerensky with a set of reforms which would enable the government to restore order as Kerensky had said. Having finished his speech, the commander-in-chief left for the train station and sped off to headquarters, while his crowd continued to give him a standing ovation.

Kerensky had spent much of 1917 maneuvering between right and left. This balancing act had so far been successful and propelled him to the national leadership. Over the course of the year, however, the political center that Kerensky occupied diminished in size every day, and Kerensky was forced to make difficult choices. Through his order to suppress the Petrograd Soviet, Kornilov had thrown down a gauntlet and forced Kerensky to take sides between the Soviet on the one hand and the liberals and conservatives on the other. Vladimir Lvov, an Octobrist politician who was a former minister in the Provisional Government, approached Kerensky and warned him of an assassination plot by Kornilov's officers. He also offered to act as an envoy between Kerensky and Kornilov in an effort to reach an understanding between the two men concerning the future of the government. When Lvov arrived at headquarters, Kornilov told him that Russia could not survive without a military dictatorship. He went on to say that he was prepared to serve under Kerensky but would prefer to take power as military dictator himself. When Lvov returned to Petrograd, he told the Prime Minister that Kornilov had aspirations to become military dictator, neglecting to mention that he was also willing to serve under Kerensky. Lvov also made the revelation that he had overheard one of Kornilov's officers speaking about assassinating Kerensky.

Lvov's report convinced Kerensky that Kornilov was up to no good. The two men exchanged telegrams but Kerensky received no clarification about Kornilov's plans. On the morning of 27 August, Kerensky sent Kornilov a telegram informing him of his dismissal from the supreme command with instructions to report to Petrograd alone. At a meeting with his ministers he informed them of Kornilov's dismissal and demanded dictatorial powers. Almost all the ministers agreed except the Kadets, who threatened to resign. Kerensky was urged not to publicize Kornilov's dismissal until a suitable solution was found. These efforts to negotiate were in vain once it became clear the Kerensky had issued a telegram to the army stating that Kornilov was a traitor. Meanwhile, Krymov's troops continued marching on Petrograd, throwing Kerensky and his government into a panic. Kornilov must have rated his chances highly, being fully aware that he had the majority of the army on his side.

Naturally, Kerensky felt threatened by the imminent prospect of men in uniform rushing into his capital under instructions from a general whom he had recently denounced as a traitor. The urgent assistance he desperately needed came from the Petrograd Soviet. Although the Soviet had been targeted by Kerensky, its leaders knew that the consequences would be much worse if they stood by idly as Kornilov's men entered Petrograd. Keen to make use of all the assistance he could find, Kerensky released senior Bolsheviks, including Trotsky and Lev Kamenev who were imprisoned following the July Days. The Bolsheviks, Mensheviks, and SRs persuaded a coordinated strategy which aimed to mobilize rail workers to sabotage the railway tracks in order to impede the progress of the trains carrying Kornilov's troops to the capital. Other socialist activists infiltrated into Kornilov's army in an effort to persuade them to desert. The Petrograd Soviet established a Military Revolutionary Committee, which distributed weapons to arm the workers against Kornilov's 'counter-revolutionary activities.' The weapons were not needed. Krymov's men found progress difficult in the midst of all the impediments the workers had placed in their path, and increasing numbers of men deserted, disdaining the prospect of taking up arms against their fellow citizens. Having been abandoned by his army, Krymov committed suicide on 31 August. Days later, Kornilov was arrested at headquarters, officially stripped of his position as commander-in-chief and imprisoned in the nearby Bykhov Monastery along with a number of other officers who participated in the coup.

The Kornilov Affair, as the attempted coup was subsequently known, further damaged the credibility of the Kerensky government. The Prime Minister dismissed much of his inner circle and established a new government called the Directorate, a conscious or unconscious echo of the Directory, the government formed by moderates during the French Revolution in 1794 following the excesses of Jacobin rule under Maximilien Robespierre. In the process, Kerensky also dissolved the State Duma and officially declared Russia a republic, eliminating any prospects of Grand Duke Mikhail eventually assuming his brother's throne. Kerensky was afraid that the continued possibility of Russia remaining a monarchy might encourage efforts by conservatives to restore the Romanovs to the throne by force. Unlike its French namesake, this Russian Directorate lasted a mere three months as Kerensky found himself increasingly bereft of allies.

The events of July and August 1917 significantly undermined Kerensky's balancing act. His decision to crack down on the Bolsheviks following the July Days damaged his credibility with the left, who believed he was in league with Kornilov to suppress the Petrograd Soviet up to the very last minute. By choosing to confront Kornilov at the crucial moment, Kerensky also lost the support of liberals and conservatives on the right, who believed that Kornilov was simply acting on orders from Kerensky himself. Kerensky hoped to solve the Provisional Government's perennial problem of being a temporary institution by granting himself more authority, but by this point it was already too late. Kerensky may have assumed greater powers, at least in name, but he was no longer in a position to use it effectively. The Kornilov Affair had a significant effect on his mental state, and he appears to have been suffering from bipolar disorder. Rumors spread around the city that the sleepless Prime Minister was wandering around the former imperial apartments in the early hours of the morning taking drugs and singing opera arias. This may have been a fabrication, but judging from his public appearance everyone could see that Kerensky was a broken man.

The net effect of the Kornilov Affair was a significant increase in support for the Bolshevik Party. The Bolsheviks made a significant contribution to the defense of Petrograd, and the Petrograd Soviet demanded Kerensky release several hundred Bolshevik activists who had been detained since the July Days. Bolshevik representation in the soviets increased during the immediate aftermath of the Kornilov Affair. Since workers and soldiers could recall their representatives at any time, the Bolsheviks took advantage of growing opposition to the Soviet's moderate policies and managed to elect Bolshevik deputies to the Petrograd Soviet. On 1 September, the Bolsheviks, who had obtained a majority in the Petrograd Soviet, forced a vote on the question of whether the soviets should assume power. It passed 700 to 13, with 36 abstentions. The Soviet's leadership under Tsereteli, however, refused to pursue this course, arguing that the vote was called at short notice. Nevertheless, he privately recognized that the tide was turning in Lenin's favor. The conditions for a Bolshevik takeover were met.

Chapter 7 – Ten Days that Shook the World

The Kornilov Affair and its consequences significantly altered the balance of political power in Petrograd. The Provisional Government and Kerensky were on its last legs, while the Petrograd Soviet, increasingly dominated by Bolsheviks, became increasingly assertive. In order to resolve the dispute that had arisen after the Soviet voted to take power against the wishes of its leadership, the All-Russian Central Executive Committee established a Democratic Conference with representation from across the country to discuss the matter. After much deliberation, the body proposed establishing a legislative body called the Provisional Council, with representatives from both the workers and the bourgeoisie. It also called for the All-Russian Congress of Soviets to convene at the end of October. On 21 September, the Bolshevik Party's Central Committee held a meeting among delegates to the Democratic Conference on the question of the party's participation in the Provisional Council. In an intense debate, hardliners led by Trotsky threatened to walk out of the Conference, while moderates such as Kamenev favored participation. The debates were an echo of those in April on the theoretical question of whether the Bolshevik Party should seize power immediately or to support the development of the bourgeois state.

When the issue was put to the floor for a vote, the moderates scored a victory with 77 votes to 50. Accordingly, the Bolsheviks agreed to participate in the Provisional Council, albeit with the intention of using their votes to prevent a coalition with the bourgeoisie. Nevertheless, Trotsky's hardline stance was supported by Lenin, who at this time was still in hiding in Finland. He writes in support of Trotsky, stating "we cannot and must not under any circumstances reconcile ourselves to participation. A group at one of the conferences is not the highest organ of the party and even the decisions of the highest organs are subject to revision on the basis of experience. We must strive at all cost to have the boycott question solved at a plenary meeting of the Central Committee and at an extraordinary party congress." By adopting this position, Lenin hoped to bypass the executive organs of his party and mobilize the party rank-and-file to support a boycott of the Council. "We must go out to the Soviets of workers, soldiers and peasants' deputies, go out into the trade unions, go out in general to the masses." The situation in Petrograd was the same as throughout the country, in Moscow, in Kiev. The party leadership favored participation, but the membership was overwhelmingly in favor of the boycott. The Bolshevik leadership in the absence of Lenin nevertheless continued their policy of engagement with the Council.

In any event, the Provisional Council lacked the political powers the moderate socialists envisaged it would have, and Kerensky refused to be held to account to the body. On 24 September, he established another coalition government with Kadets and socialists, although the political talent of these new ministers was significantly limited. Kerensky hoped that this government would at least keep him going until November, when the elections to the Constituent Assembly were to be held. Kerensky's refusal to be accountable to the Provisional Council was a sign that the moderate socialist parties had also run out of ideas. Both the Mensheviks and the SRs experienced a drastic decline in popular support at the expensive of their Bolshevik rivals. On 25 September, the Bolsheviks were confident enough to challenge for the leadership of the Petrograd Soviet. They called for the executive to be replaced, observing that Kerensky remained a member of the Soviet's executive, even though the majority of the deputies now regarded him as a counter-revolutionary. The body duly elected Leon Trotsky as Chairman of the Petrograd Soviet in place of the Menshevik incumbent, Nikolai Chkeidze.

Despite this resolution, Lenin, still hiding in the Finnish city of Vyborg, continued to urge the Bolshevik leadership to take power immediately and form a Bolshevik government, before the Congress was convened to sanction the action. He saw no future in forming a coalition government with the SRs and Mensheviks, even if this was done through the soviets. While Trotsky agreed with Lenin's uncompromising stance, he preferred to wait until the Congress for the seizure of power. Other senior leaders, including Kamenev and Zinoviev, refused to consider any seizure of power and preferred to form a coalition government with the other socialist parties. In his letters to the party's Central Committee, Lenin voiced fears that if they did not act immediately, Kerensky would crack down on the Bolsheviks and suppress the Constituent Assembly. Perhaps the bourgeois elements in the government would surrender Petrograd, which was in any case full of troublesome socialists, to the Germans. This was unlikely. Instead, Lenin knew that should the Soviet vote to take power, the inevitable result would be a coalition government between the Bolsheviks, Mensheviks, and SRs, even if the Bolsheviks would be the largest party. The leader of this government would most likely be Kamenev, who championed a policy of compromise with the moderates. Lenin could only ensure that he became head of government if the Bolsheviks were to take power before the Congress met.

In order to make his case to the party leadership, Lenin decided to return to Petrograd in disguise. He convened a meeting of the

Central Committee on 10 October to discuss the question of taking power. Only twelve members out of twenty-one were present at the fateful meeting. The debate was intense, with Kamenev and Zinoviev speaking against an insurrection. By the end of the meeting, a vote was taken. The Central Committee voted ten to two in favor of an armed insurrection, with only Kamenev and Zinoviev voting against. Once again, through sheer force of personality Lenin had managed to convince his fellow party leaders of the necessity for seizing power. Nevertheless, the debate did not address the issue of timing. Lenin still had to persuade his comrades that time was of the essence.

Lenin continued to agitate among the leadership for an immediate insurrection. On 16 October he called another meeting of the Central Committee, to which representatives of the Bolshevik Military Committee were invited, and proposed that the planned armed action should take place before the Congress convened in Petrograd on 20 October. Despite warnings from the military committee that there were many obstacles to a seizure of power, Lenin was unwavering in his determination to pursue an immediate insurrection. When this was put to a vote, Lenin won fifteen to six, demonstrating that not only Kamenev and Zinoviev were concerned about the risks involved in the attempt to seize power. After losing the vote, Kamenev said he could not accept the resolution and would resign from the party, believing that the insurrection would lead the party to ruin. On 18 October, Kamenev and Zinoviev published a piece in Maxim Gorky's paper *Novaya Zhizn'*, referring to the internal party debates and spoke for the need of a socialist coalition government instead of a pure Bolshevik government.

Lenin was incensed at this development, denouncing the two men as traitors to the revolution. By publishing their letter, Kamenev and Zinoviev made the planned Bolshevik insurrection public knowledge and gave both the Soviet and the Provisional Government time to prepare. The Soviet postponed the Congress until 25 October, hoping to gather its forces and prepare for the Bolshevik challenge.

In fact, this delay allowed the Bolsheviks to make their final preparations. A Military Revolutionary Committee (MRC) was set up by Trotsky to oversee the logistics of the operation. Moderate socialists in the Soviet demanded that Trotsky declare the true intention of the Bolsheviks. Trotsky denied that any insurrection was in the works, but his answers were evasive and his performance was unconvincing. Meanwhile, Kerensky remained optimistic. He sought to provoke the Bolsheviks by sending troops from the Petrograd garrison to the front, and on the morning of 24 October ordered loyal troops to take action against the Bolsheviks, giving instructions to close two Bolshevik newspapers. Kerensky also ordered reinforcements from the front, forging the signatures of Soviet leaders since he doubted they would respond to the orders of the Provisional Government alone.

In response, Trotsky put the MRC on standby but did not give the green light for insurrection, since he first hoped to receive the Soviet's support for the action. He described the action as the first steps of a counter-revolution against the Petrograd Soviet, but the moderates were not convinced. Kamenev continued his efforts to rally support for a socialist coalition government. While this was taking place, events overtook the political negotiations in the Soviet. The Red Guards were already on the move, taking control of key points of communication: railway stations, bridges, post and telegraph offices, telephone exchanges, and banks. The Red Guards had also taken over police stations. Lenin was determined to capitalize on these early successes. At 6pm he gave official sanction for the insurrection. The Soviet Congress would be meeting the following afternoon, and it was essential for the takeover to be complete by then. At 10pm, Lenin, despite fear of arrest, decided to make his way to the Smolny Institute wearing his wig with a bandage wrapped around his head. Near the Tauride Palace he was stopped by police who saw him acting suspiciously, but they soon released him for being a harmless drunk. It was a costly mistake to make.

Lenin arrived just before midnight. He was not recognized in his disguise, and he had to struggle to be admitted into the room where the Bolsheviks were deliberating on plans to seize the city. His appearance spurred the Bolshevik leaders into action. The plan was as follows. On the morning of 25 October, Red Guards, Kronstadt sailors, and loyal garrison troops would seize Mariinsky Palace and disperse the Provisional Council which met there. They would then move on to the Winter Palace. The signal for an assault would be given by the Cruiser Aurora, which steamed up the River Neva. By noon, it was expected that the Winter Palace would be taken, and the Provisional Government would fall, in time for Lenin to announce that the Bolsheviks had taken power in the name of the soviets. In practice, technical difficulties and elementary obstacles meant that after taking control of the Mariinsky Palace, the Bolshevik soldiers and sailors had to postpone their assault on the Winter Palace until the evening.

The Winter Palace was sparsely defended by a few thousand troops, including cadets, reservists, and the Women's Battalion of Death. American journalist John Reed, a Bolshevik sympathizer who later published *Ten Days that Shook the World*, his celebrated account of the revolution, reported that the defensive garrison was drunk, hungry, and resigned to defeat. In fact, most of the soldiers assigned to guard the Winter Palace had left for dinner and never returned. The order for the assault finally came at 9:45pm, with the Kronstadt sailors firing a blank shell from the Aurora. Artillery stationed at the Peter and Paul Fortress on the other side of the Neva fired shells at the palace. The Red Guards entered through a side staircase, while the ministers of the Provisional Government hid in a dining room and waited for the inevitable. Kerensky was not among them, having left for headquarters in the morning in an effort to locate the troops he requested. Sometime after 2am on 26 October, after searching hundreds of rooms of the palace, the Red Guards finally found the ministers and placed them under arrest. The Bolsheviks had overthrown the Provisional Government.

At 10:40pm, while the Red Guards were still in the process of seizing the Winter Palace, the Second All-Russian Congress of Soviets opened at the Smolny Institute. The Bolsheviks, together with their Left SR allies, had a small majority in the Congress. This was not an entirely accurate representation of Bolshevik support across the country, but superior organization by the party allowed them to elect more delegates. As the meeting was underway, Mensheviks and moderate SRs denounced the Bolsheviks for the actions that had taken place, arguing that counter-revolution was inevitable and all the gains made since February were at risk. The moderates walked out of the hall, declaring that they would have nothing to do with the 'criminal venture' that the Bolsheviks were undertaking. As they filed out of the congress hall, Trotsky mocked them with a famous denunciation: "You are pitiful isolated individuals; you are bankrupts; your role is played out. Go where you belong from now on—into the dustbin of history!" The walkout meant that the Bolsheviks were left with a huge majority when the question of the seizure of power was taken to a vote. The transfer of power to the Bolsheviks was thus officially sanctioned by the Soviet.

Chapter 8 – Peace, Land, and Bread

The armed insurrection which brought the Bolsheviks to power was a relatively modest affair. Unlike the hundreds of thousands of workers, soldiers, and sailors who gathered on the streets in February and July, no more than 25,000 men took part in the assault on the Winter Palace. When the citizens of Petrograd woke up on the morning of 26 October, there was nothing to suggest that power had changed hands. Nevertheless, developments at the Smolny Institute would have significant repercussions for Russia's political future.

Lenin and his fellow Bolsheviks began to sketch out the structure of the new government even before the armed insurrection succeeded. Gathered around Bolshevik Party headquarters at the Smolny, they deliberated on what to call their new government. They were not keen on calling themselves ministers since this would give them the air of bourgeois respectability which they rejected outright. At length, they accepted Trotsky's suggestion of 'people's commissars,' which was inspired by Jacobin France. The new government was therefore called the Council of People's Commissars (Sovnarkom) with Lenin as Chairman and head of government. Key posts were given to senior leaders. Trotsky became People's Commissar for

Foreign Affairs, Rykov—Internal Affairs, Lunacharsky—Education, Stalin—Nationalities. Alexandra Kollontai, the only female member of Lenin's government, became People's Commissar for Social Welfare. Significantly, neither Kamenev nor Zinoviev were given portfolios in the government, although the Bolshevized Soviet Congress did elect Kamenev as Chairman of the All-Russian Central Executive Committee, effectively head of state. The party remained divided and Kamenev did not believe Lenin's government would last for more than a couple of weeks.

Once in control of the government, Lenin was faced with the task not only of transforming Russia into a socialist state but also addressing the numerous political issues that the Provisional Government had failed to address, which eventually led to its downfall. On 26 October, Lenin presented two decrees on peace and land to the Soviet Congress, which dutifully passed them. The Decree on Peace signaled to the participants in the First World War that a 'just and democratic peace' should be made between the warring nations without territorial or financial compensation. At the same time, Lenin echoed US President Woodrow Wilson's call for national self-determination. National units within larger political entities should have the right to independence. Lenin called for an armistice to be agreed upon immediately between the two sides and for negotiations to take place as part of a peace conference. Perhaps more radically, Lenin declared that the new Bolshevik government would publicize the secret clauses and agreements made between Russian and foreign diplomats during the Tsarist and Provisional governments. This was a major departure from centuries of secret diplomacy in Russia as in the rest of Europe. Negotiations were opened with the Germans and ended with the Treaty of Brest-Litovsk, signed in March 1918. Despite its punitive terms, Lenin believed he was taking one step back in order to take two steps forward in an effort to consolidate the Soviet power.

The second decree, the Decree on Land, addressed the question of land redistribution, an issue of particular concern to the peasantry over the course of 1917. Although the SRs continued to enjoy high levels of popularity among the peasantry, their failure to take any action on the question resulted in a decline in support, especially in urban centers. Lenin's decree abolished the property rights of the imperial family, the aristocracy, and the Russian Orthodox Church, transferring ownership of the land to peasant committees and Soviets. It is worth noting that the decree resembled SR policy far more than it did Bolshevik policy, which envisaged that all land would be transferred to state ownership. Lenin recognized that the Bolsheviks lacked support in the countryside and in order to gain control of the whole country, the Bolsheviks had to give some concessions to the peasants. Of course, the fact that Lenin was now operating the levers of power meant that once the Bolsheviks were to consolidate their power in the countryside, the policy could be changed at any moment and Lenin's government could decide appropriate the land from the peasants for the state.

Another key issue for Lenin's government was the fate of the ethnic minorities in the Russian Empire. Communist doctrine stated that national entities should be allowed to determine their own fates, and one of the elements of Lenin's Decree on Peace was to this effect. However, when the question turned to Russia, the Bolsheviks were in a difficult position. The periphery of the Russian Empire included key economic resources, without which Russia would be impoverished. Ukraine in particular was the breadbasket of the Russian Empire, and in times of peace provided the rest of the country with abundant quantities of grain. In 1913 Stalin published the theoretical work *Marxism and the National Question*, which concluded that the grievances of minorities lay not in the lack of independence but the lack of autonomy, especially on linguistic, educational, and cultural matters. Lenin supported Stalin's position on the issue and regarded him as the leading theoretician on the national issue, which led to his appointment as People's Commissar of the Nationalities. Nevertheless, when the issue came to a debate among the people's commissars on 2 November, the government declared that ethnic minorities had the right to break away and become fully independent. This declaration was made despite Lenin and Stalin's opposition, suggesting that the Sovnarkom was by no means Lenin's one-man show.

As Marxists, Lenin's government was also keen to create an equal society. On 10 November, the government abolished legal distinctions of privilege, including titles and ranks. This was a major development in the structure of Russian society. The Table of Ranks, which had been introduced by Peter the Great in 1722 in order to create a meritocratic culture in the army and government but was subsequently used to for purposes of social distinction among the higher echelons of Russian society, was abolished by Lenin. Instead, every man, woman, and child would become a citizen of Russian Republic. The convoluted forms of address which accompanied the Table of Ranks were also eliminated. Instead, men and women would address each other simply as 'citizen' or 'comrade.' The former greeting had been in common use since the February Revolution, but the Bolsheviks preferred 'comrade' as a result of their proletarian instincts. Over the subsequent months, courts became democratically elected and ranks within the army were abolished.

The policies pursued by Sovnarkom immediately after the revolution appeared to reflect their intentions to create a free and fair society. However, a much darker side to Bolshevik rule also began to emerge. Few expected the Bolshevik government to last long, and there were many elements of society irreconciled to the continued prospect of Bolshevik rule. It should also be stressed that taking power in Petrograd did not mean taking control of the whole of Russia. It took ten days for the Bolsheviks to seize control of Moscow, and large parts of southern Russia declared in favor of right-wing Cossack generals. Kerensky himself was gathering troops to retake Petrograd, and the influential railway union argued that the socialist parties should cooperate to face the challenge, as it had done during the Kornilov Affair, or face the prospect of defeat. Lenin sent Bolsheviks to negotiate with the unions, but the defeat of

Kerensky's forces at the Pulkovo Heights to the south of Petrograd meant that the Bolsheviks were no longer interested. In the meantime, Lenin gave orders to close down newspapers not only of the liberal bourgeoisie but also of rival socialist parties, which caused outrage among the Mensheviks and SRs as well as moderate Bolsheviks. Lenin was keen to transform the Russian Republic into a one-party state.

The socialist opposition to the Bolsheviks placed their hopes in the elections to the Constituent Assembly in the hope that this would dilute Bolshevik influence in the country's political institutions. The Constituent Assembly had been envisaged from March as the supreme representative institution that would decide on key constitutional and political issues that faced the country. The closest antecedent in Russia was the Assembly of the Land summoned in 1612 to elect a new tsar after the extinction of the previous ruling dynasty. Despite the Bolshevik seizure of power, Lenin did not move to abolish the Constituent Assembly and allowed elections to take place as planned. Official statements from Sovnarkom recognized the supreme authority of the forthcoming assembly. Indeed, the Bolsheviks campaigned passionately all around the country as polling took place, including among soldiers at the front, over the course of several weeks in November.

It soon became clear that the Bolsheviks would not only fail to win a majority in the new assembly but that it would not even emerge as the largest party. When the final results were declared, the Socialist Revolutionaries won an impressive 40 percent of the vote and a majority in terms of seats, demonstrating that it retained much of its support from the Russian countryside. The Bolsheviks came in second place with 24 percent, while the Mensheviks gained 3 percent. The Kadets, conservatives, and nationalist parties polled in the single digits. The SR victory in the elections to the Constituent Assembly undermined Lenin's claims that the Bolsheviks had taken power on behalf of the people. On closer inspection, however, the Bolsheviks did perform very strongly among the urban proletariat, which was always going to be the active force in a Marxist revolution. In Petrograd and Moscow, the Bolsheviks won a little less than 50 percent of the vote and also recorded large majorities among soldiers at the front.

The fact that the Bolsheviks did not receive the level of support they expected hardened Bolshevik attitudes towards the Constituent Assembly. Lenin claimed that the SRs could not command a majority in the assembly since the party had split into two separate factions, the Left and Right SRs, in the summer. The assembly was scheduled to be convened on 28 November, but that morning Kronstadt sailors carried out the arrest of the Kadet deputies on Sovnarkom's orders and postponed the opening of the assembly until January 1918. When the assembly finally met on 5 January at the Tauride Palace, it elected Viktor Chernov as chairman and voted to reject the Lenin's decrees on land and peace, endorsing SR proposals instead. At 1am the Bolsheviks walked out of the meeting, describing the body as serving the interests of the counter-revolution. The meeting adjourned at 6am, but by the time the deputies returned at noon they were denied entry and informed that the assembly had been shut down by the Council of People's Commissars.

Lenin justified his action by arguing that Constituent Assembly had been established by the Provisional Government and therefore represented bourgeois interests. Since the Soviet had already taken power in October, there was no longer any need for the Constituent Assembly. Although relegated to a footnote of the narrative of the events of the revolution by many historians, the suppression of the Constituent Assembly represented a pivotal moment in both the revolution and Russian history in as a whole. The opposition to the Bolsheviks could no longer count on representative institutional bodies to challenge Bolshevik authority. Civil war was inescapable. It would not be a simple class war between socialists on one side and capitalists on the other. Instead, the Bolsheviks and their fellow socialist parties would fight on different sides, if not necessarily on opposite sides.

Chapter 9 – Defending the Revolution

At the beginning of 1918 the Bolsheviks consolidated their control of Petrograd, but there was still much to do in terms of extending their authority across the whole country. Russian soldiers were still fighting in the war and feared that Petrograd would fall to the Germans. In March, the capital was relocated to Moscow. After its suppression in Petrograd, the Constituent Assembly relocated to the Siberian city of Samara on the Volga and set up a rival government. In the south, a number of right-wing monarchist generals and their armies raised their banners in an effort to crush the Bolshevik government. These forces gradually coalesced into the White movement, although coordination between the generals was difficult to achieve due to personal animosities and geographical distance. In 1918 and 1919, three White armies, supported by small contingents of foreign troops, converged on the capital of Moscow. The largest force was commanded by Admiral Alexander Kolchak, who had captured Samara and taken control of the moderate socialist government. Kolchak, already in control of much of Siberia, therefore assumed the title of Supreme Leader. General Anton Denikin's army approached Moscow from the south, while General Nikolai Yudenich's army threatened Petrograd from the southwest. The lack of coordination between the three armies meant that the Bolsheviks were able to defeat all of them in turn. By the end of

1919, the Bolsheviks gained control of much of Russia, and it was only left to drive out the remnants of Denikin's army under the command of Baron Pyotr Wrangel in the south.

The Bolsheviks enjoyed a number of key advantages which allowed them to defeat the White armies. Most obviously, they could count on greater manpower. While the White armies were able to field several hundred thousand men, the Red Army managed to field five million over the course of the war. The Red Army, under Trotsky's leadership, was far more effectively led and organized than the Whites. The most important factor in the Reds' successes was not political but geographical. The Bolsheviks controlled Russia's European heartland, where its industry and population was concentrated. The center was well connected by railways compared to the periphery, which allowed the Bolsheviks to transport armies from one front to another depending on which sector was under the greatest danger. The Whites were also operating from territory that was not ethnically Russian and refused to give concessions to non-Russian national entities. Although the Reds also had to fight national independence movements, most significantly the Anarchist Green Army of Nestor Makhno in Ukraine, they were far more prepared to grant concessions of autonomy in exchange for support among the local population in the regions.

The Civil War was accompanied by an increase in repressive measures imposed by the Bolshevik state in its own territory. Fearful that bourgeois elements could rise in support of the approaching White armies, the Bolsheviks aimed to eliminate class enemies. The highest profile of these victims included members of the imperial family. On 17 July, Citizen Nicholas Romanov, the former Tsar Nicholas II, was executed in the Siberian city of Ekaterinburg alongside his wife, five children, and four servants. Grand Duke Mikhail, who had refused the throne on grounds of personal safety, had been killed in June. Several close relations of the imperial family were also killed, although Nicholas II's two sisters Xenia and Olga managed to survive and escaped to the west, along with their mother

Dowager Empress Maria Fyodorovna. The Bolshevik's stepped up their repressive measures in September. This was largely the consequence of an assassination attempt on Lenin by the disenchanted Socialist Revolutionary Fanya Kaplan. Between September and October over 100,000 people of all classes and political backgrounds fell victim to a repressive campaign known as the Red Terror. This campaign of repression was orchestrated by the Cheka, the Bolshevik secret police headed by the Polish communist Felix Dzerzhinsky.

By 1921, the Civil War was over, and it seemed as though the victorious Bolsheviks had successfully consolidated their grip on power. However, it was precisely at this point that Lenin faced a series of new challenges from within his enlarged state. The punitive measures imposed on the Soviet population during the war was met with hostility by peasants, who engaged in clashes with Red Army soldiers over the course of the war. By March 1921 the Bolsheviks had lost control of much of the countryside. At the same time, demonstrations in Petrograd over food shortages inspired a mutiny of the Kronstadt sailors. The Kronstadt sailors had been among the most enthusiastic champions of the October Revolution, but the authoritarian manner in which the Bolshevik commissars behaved angered the sailors. Opposition to Lenin was also apparent within the party itself in the form of the Workers' Opposition and the Democratic Centralists, two factions which opposed Lenin's policy.

Lenin addressed these three particular issues within the space of a couple of weeks in March 1921. The occasion was the Tenth Party Congress, which opened on 8 March. At the party congress, Lenin announced a ban on factions, which ensured that the party would be united behind Lenin in the future. On 15 October, as the Congress was about to close, Lenin dispatched a military force of 50,000 men under Trotsky to suppress the rebellion, marching across the frozen Gulf of Finland to the Kronstadt naval base. After eighteen hours of fighting, the mutineers were crushed and the survivors taken into captivity. Most significant of all, at the party congress Lenin introduced a radical new economic policy under the unoriginal title of New Economic Policy. Lenin believed that the peasant threat was far greater than that posed by the White armies, and he granted concessions to the peasantry in an effort to regain control of the countryside. He introduced a limited free market in the countryside and ordered an end to the food requisitioning that had been in place during the Civil War. Although the 'commanding heights' of the economy would remain under state ownership, it was a radical departure from the previous policy of War Communism, which claimed all produce for the state. The adoption of the NEP as a tactical retreat on the policy front showed that the Bolsheviks were still a long way from fulfilling all the revolutionary objectives.

Conclusion

On 9 March 1923, Lenin suffered the third of three major strokes which left him incapacitated and unable to play a part in government. He finally died on 21 January 1924, mourned by all around him as the leader of the Great October Socialist Revolution, without which the Soviet government would not have existed. His body was later embalmed and placed in a mausoleum on Red Square, where it continues to lie to this day. Lenin's lieutenants already began struggling for power before his death, and after his death these power struggles became public. Trotsky, who was in many ways Lenin's natural successor, was sidelined by his rivals in the Politburo. The man who would eventually emerge victorious was Bolshevik Party General Secretary Josef Stalin, who would rule the Soviet Union until his death in 1953.

During his five years in power Lenin managed to set in motion a complete transformation of Soviet society. He abolished privilege and established equality in law for all Soviet citizens. He moved the capital to Moscow from Petrograd, which was renamed Leningrad after his death. More fundamentally, he changed the Russian language, removing obsolete letters from the Cyrillic alphabet. He changed the calendar, adopting the Gregorian Calendar at the expense of the Julian Calendar, which continues to be used by the Russian Orthodox Church. The Bolsheviks launched an anti-religious campaign which forced the Orthodox Church underground.

Lenin's government championed *avant garde* art and literature at the expense of the more restrained bourgeois tastes.

The political events which had taken place in Russia over the course of 1917 had an equally significant impact on the rest of the world. Soviet Russia, from 1922 the Soviet Union, was the first socialist state in history. Although Lenin and Trotsky failed in their attempts to export the revolution to the rest of Europe after the failure to defeat an independent Polish state in the Russo-Polish War of 1920-21, Communist regimes eventually emerged in Eastern Europe, Latin America, Asia, and Africa. The struggle between capitalism, nationalism, and communism defined much of twentieth-century international relations. The Cold War never saw the United States and the Soviet Union come into direct conflict with one another, but proxy wars in Korea and Vietnam caused much bitterness and bloodshed, leaving an important legacy in the United States. The Soviet invasion of Afghanistan and Cold War dynamics in the Middle East continue to have repercussions to this day.

Yet for all the changes the Bolsheviks brought to Russia and the world, how much did Russian society fundamentally change? For all of the Bolsheviks' egalitarian instincts, Soviet society was undoubtedly hierarchical. A small group of Soviet political elites replaced the old aristocracy, retaining access to luxury items from the west even as these items were absent from stores in Moscow and Leningrad. Much like the tsarist Okhrana, the Bolsheviks had their own secret police, the Cheka, which later morphed into the NKVD and the KGB. Lenin and Stalin demonstrated that they could be as bloody, and usually far more so, as any Romanov tsar. The Soviet state was not as atheistic as it seemed. The cult of Lenin assumed a Messianic character. The banners of Lenin and Stalin, Marx and Engels, which were displayed prominently during Soviet political rallies, were reminiscent of religious icons. The Red Sun of Communism was an echo of pagan belief that remained part of the religious landscape in rural Russia.

The collapse of the Romanov dynasty and the coming to power of the Bolsheviks is often considered historically inevitable. Yet just because a historical event happened does not necessarily mean it was inevitable. The events covered in this book show that there were a number of contingent factors which led to the Bolshevik seizure of power in 1917. The Tsarist state, although under heavy pressure in the beginning of the 20th century, only collapsed due to the political and economic pressure in Petrograd caused by the First World War. Even after Nicholas decided to abdicate, it was conceivable that his son Alexei could continue ruling at the head of a constitutional monarchy.

The Provisional Government that emerged following the February Revolution was subjected to both internal and external pressure, forced to navigate the narrow path between left and right while remaining committed to the Allied cause in the war. Nevertheless, it almost survived until the Constituent Assembly elections. It is clear that without Lenin's uncompromising stance in opposition to the Provisional Government, as well his insistence that the Bolsheviks should launch an insurrection before the Soviet decided to take power, the nature of the government would have been very different, most likely a coalition government between the SRs, Mensheviks, and Bolsheviks. Once the Bolsheviks had taken power in October, it took them almost four years to consolidate it.

Looking back on the tumultuous events of 1917, Soviet propaganda gave the impression that the Bolsheviks easily took power in October on a wave of popular support. Without Lenin at the helm of the party, the Bolsheviks would never have taken power, at least not on its on accord and not in 1917. As this book seeks to demonstrate, Lenin's path to power was far more complicated than it seems.

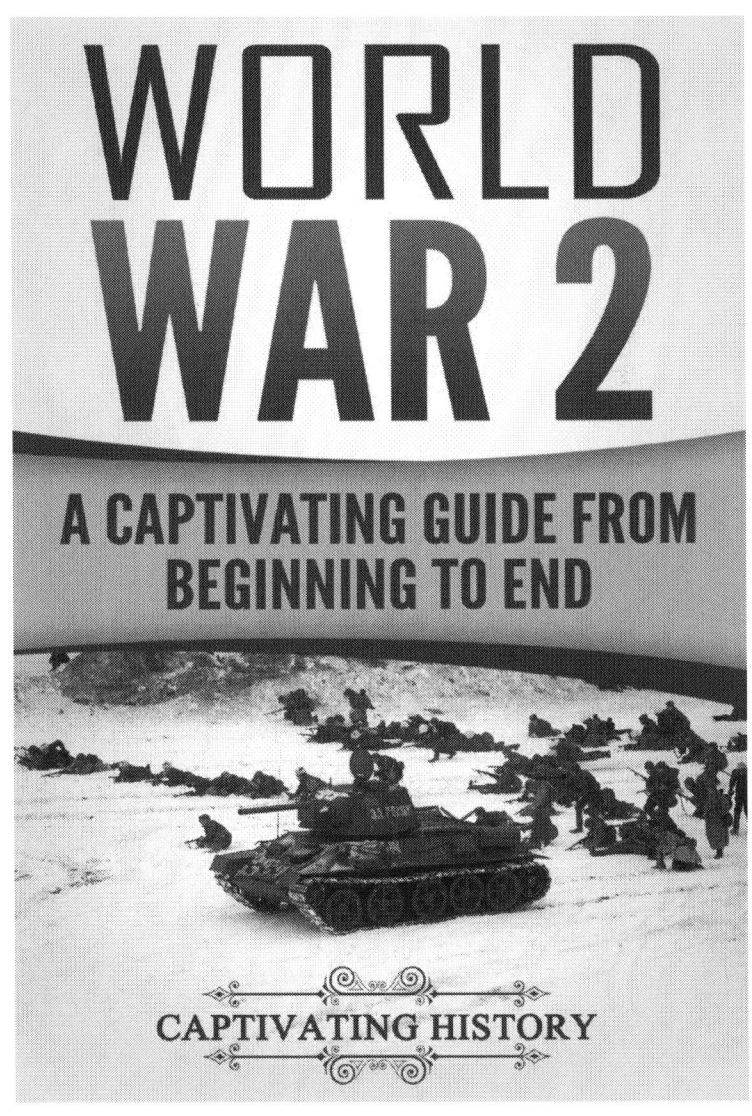

WORLD WAR 2

A CAPTIVATING GUIDE FROM BEGINNING TO END

CAPTIVATING HISTORY

Check out this book!

Check out this book!

Check out this book!

Check out this book!

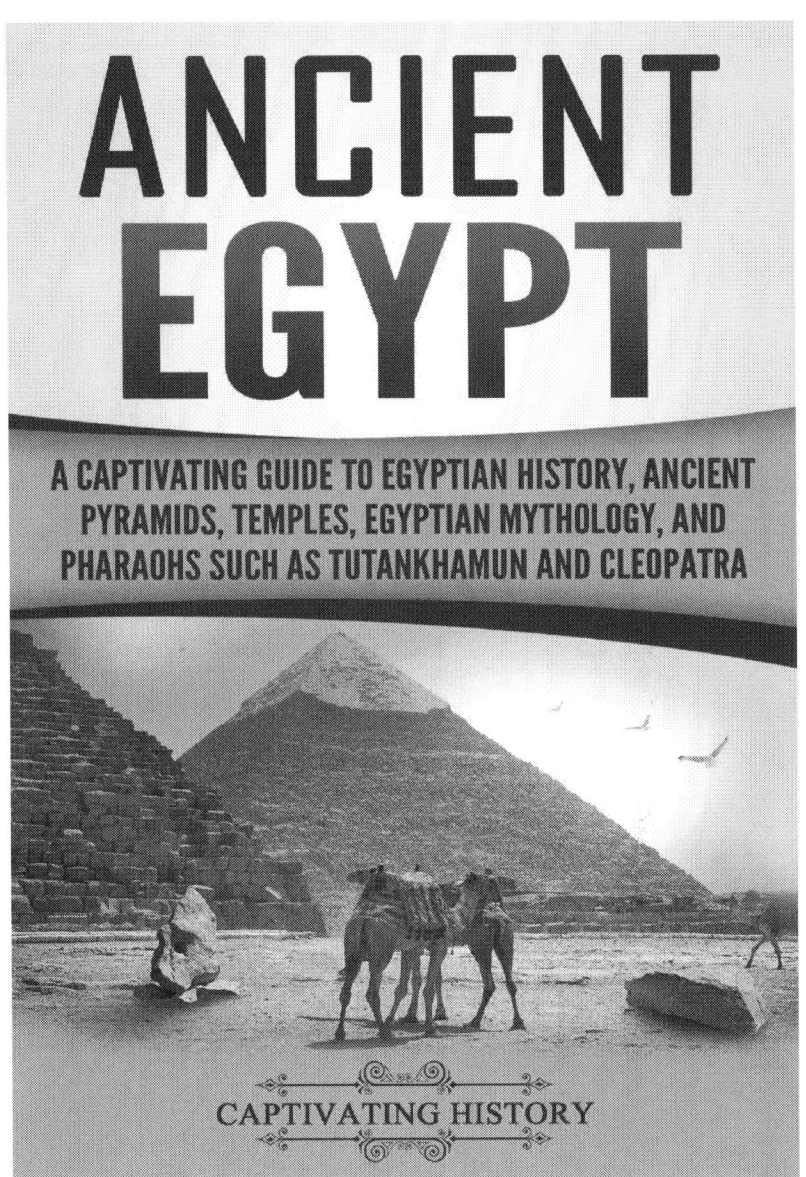

Check out this book!

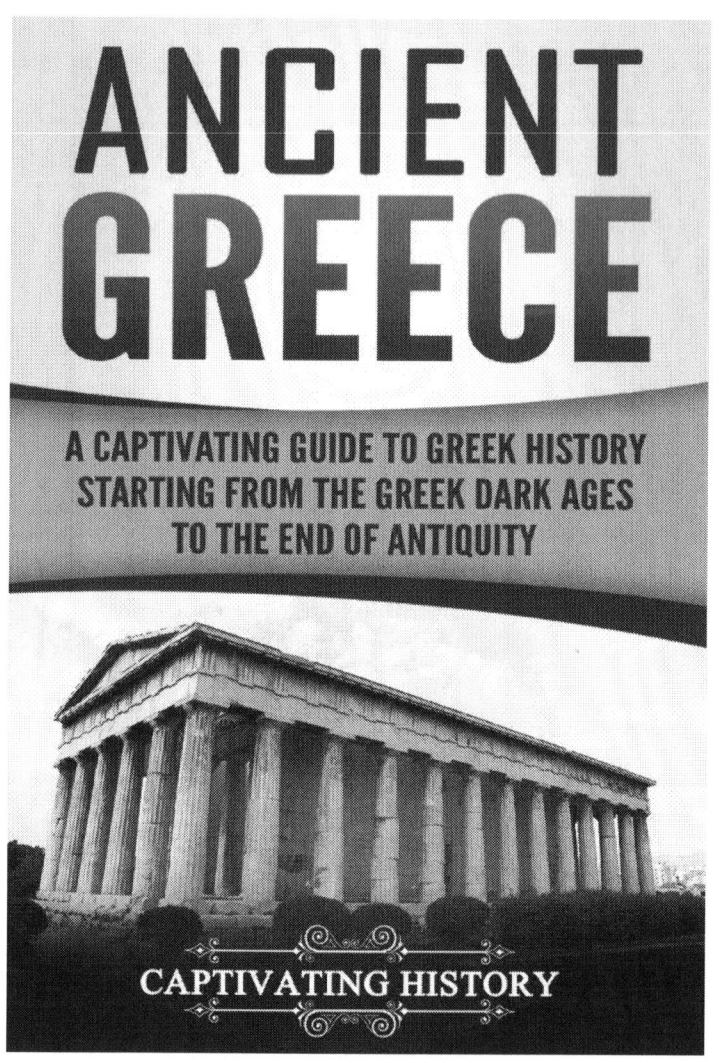

Check out this book!

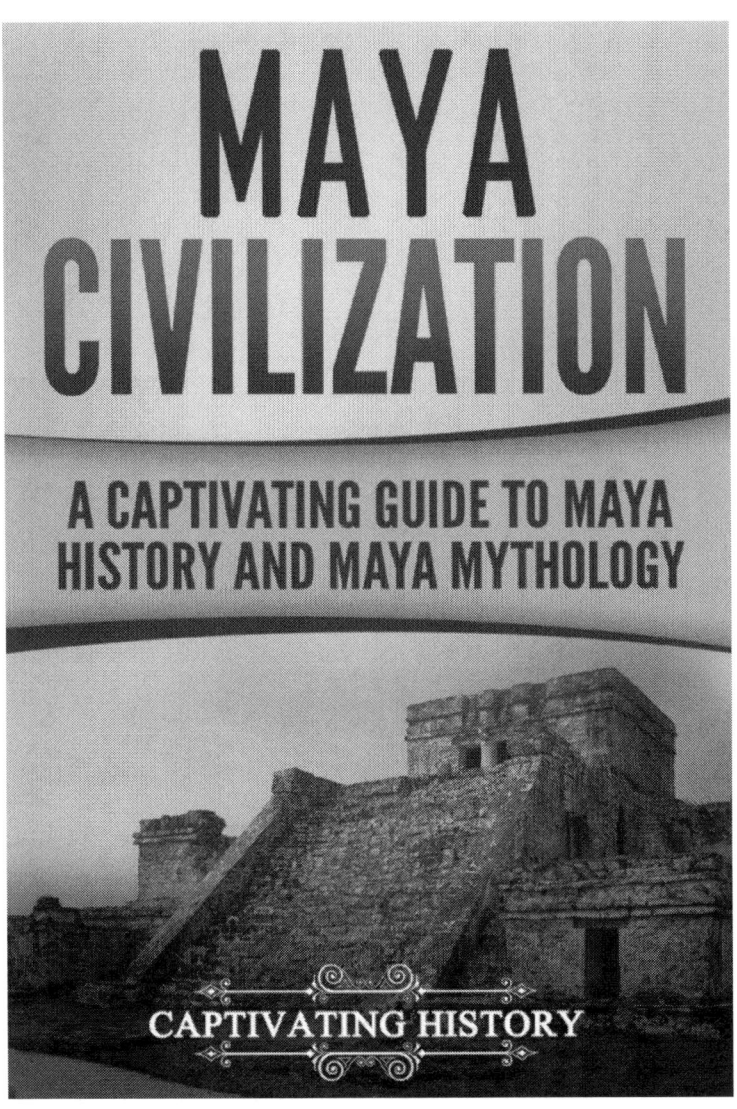

Check out this book!

Further Reading

Books

Acton, E., *Rethinking the Russian Revolution* (London, 1990).

Figes, O., *A People's Tragedy: The Russian Revolution 1891-1924* (London, 1997).

Fitzpatrick, S., *The Russian Revolution* (Oxford, 2008).

Lieven, D.C.B., *Nicholas II: Emperor of All the Russias* (London, 1993).

Lieven, D.C.B., *Towards the Flame: Empire, War and the End of Tsarist Russia* (London, 2016).

Lyandres, S., *The Fall of Tsarism: Untold Stories of the February 1917 Revolution* (Oxford, 2013).

Merridale, C., *Lenin on the Train* (London, 2017).

Pipes, R., *The Russian Revolution* (London, 1992).

Rabinowitch, A., *The Bolsheviks Come to Power: The Revolution of 1917 in Petrograd* (London, 2017).

Reed, J., *Ten Days that Shook the World* (London, 1977).

Service, R., *Lenin: A Biography* (London, 2010).

Service, R., *Trotsky: A Biography* (London, 2010).

Steinberg, M.D., *Voices of Revolution, 1917,* Annals of Communism (New Haven and London, 2001).

Zygar, M., *The Empire Must Die: Russia's Revolutionary Collapse, 1900-1917* (New York, 2017).

Websites

https://1917live.red/

https://1917resources.aseees.hcommons.org/

https://www.marxists.org/history/ussr/events/revolution/

http://www.orlandofiges.info

http://spartacus-educational.com/Russian-Revolution.htm

http://web.mit.edu/russia1917/DigitalResources.html

Free Bonus from Captivating History (Available for a Limited time)

Hi History Lovers!

Now you have a chance to join our exclusive history list so you can get your first history ebook for free as well as discounts and a potential to get more history books for free! Simply visit the link below to join.

Captivatinghistory.com/ebook

Also, make sure to follow us on:

Twitter: @Captivhistory

Facebook: Captivating History:@captivatinghistory

Printed in Poland
by Amazon Fulfillment
Poland Sp. z o.o., Wrocław